The Presence

Also by Richard Bell and published by Ginninderra Press
Such Sweet Sorrow

Richard Bell

The Presence of Absence

'one's not half two, it's two are halves of one'
e.e. cummings

The Presence of Absence
ISBN 978 1 76109 412 5
Copyright © text Richard Bell 2022

First published 2022 by
GINNINDERRA PRESS
PO Box 3461 Port Adelaide 5015
www.ginninderrapress.com.au

Contents

Glenbrook Gorge

Five decades have passed since
I sat alone on the flat rocks edging that gap,
and it is as real as this present grey Melbourne day.
The sun slides down to a peaceful west,
and the five-seventeen snakes along the blue-shaded wall below,
while unseen lizards are chased by an eager black dog
through the tufted grass, and the sandstone's warmth
seeps slowly into my shadowed legs – I feel it now.

Across the gorge the ochre face of the southern wall
pushes another sunset into the curtain of anxiety
that even now, hangs before me as uncertain
as the creek waters below, breaking around rocks, now left, now right.
I throw a mental bridge across this moment, the gorge,
to the trees that fringe the clifftop of the other side.

The unknown region there, as much past as future,
where I may find 'that serene and blessed mood'
caught in the comforting Australian scent, that even here,
drifts across from eucalyptus trees – or fear,

as when trapped in a fifties Saturday matinee
by a land of dinosaurs waiting to terrify this Ballarat boy,
alongside the persecuting giggles of a row of girls,
the presence of others unknown, that now looms
in my mind, and in the shadows of a deepening dusk.

And perhaps a sudden love or loss –
as that girl, driving me across this gorge then,
and now, the death of this same woman,
driving me back again.

Seven Senryū

Such a strange feeling –
they will not be worn again,
these clothes being washed.

At the end, so sad –
death has drained the last blueness
from your open eyes.

Now here without you
I don't know that I can eat
oysters any more.

Just drying my hands
on your towel: I am you now
and you can be me.

This quiet Christmas,
the old wreath on the front door
a different meaning.

Some thousands of weeks
together, this week alone
seems just as long.

Brandied strawberries,
What could be more you than this?
More brandy, much more!

Mother of one, wife of another

On your unaware and past caring journey
away from a painful being
to simply not being,
you no longer differentiate
among the people in your hospice room:

your daughter is not distinguished
from your brother-in-law – and
your husband? He is no different
to the stand bearing the unused
blood pressure monitor.
While your sister weeps, silently.

Your painkiller pump
maintains a silent but vigilant
guardianship of your unconsciousness.
We hear nothing – and in the silence
your dying makes our living something
we suddenly need to think about.
We are frightened – so we say,
in dying, she is brave, so brave.

Beyond the billowing translucent curtains,
the distant traffic on Studley Park Road
provides an irregular pulsing beat
that could be your heart, though the traffic
will go on through the night
while we will have gone home
to resume our now diminished lives,

and your heart slowly slows, perhaps stops,
and you lie there, under the fresh uncrumpled
sheet and blanket, clad only in a nappy,
leaving this world as you entered it –
except for the wedding ring
still on your finger.

The wedding ring you always wore

At university, you always wore
a wedding ring, a wide plain gold band.
And usually on the third finger of the left hand.
Your grandmother's wedding ring, you said.

It drove me mad when I didn't know you –
but wanted to. Were you married?
How does one ask such a question? Dare one,
dare I? No way, the question would
have revealed my interest, and the answer
could have destroyed me.

But eventually you gave me that ring
to keep for thirteen days, when,
sometime after ten-thirty on a late October morning,
I put it back on the third finger of your left hand.
Where it stayed for the next forty-seven years
– except when you were revitalising
your hands with expensive creams.

Now this ring sits in a drawer,
destined for your granddaughter.
Taken from your lifeless finger
by the hospice nurse.
The edges are sharper now, like
the memories of this and other artefacts
of our lives.

Like my life
the old gold looks duller –
I shall not miss this ring. But
will it mean as much about you
to your granddaughter
as it did to you of yours?

Or as it did to me of you?

The havoc of memories

In times like these
memories disrupt our lives,
break up trains of thought and action.

I am walking from the front room
to the kitchen, and a memory of you
rearranging the flowers in the hall
robs me of knowing why
I have come to the kitchen.

Or I am talking to a neighbour about
pruning the roses, when an image of you,
clipping just opened rosebuds
for a vase in the dining room,
chokes my speech and forces tears
to the margins of my eyes.

Each time I am casually flung
between my life and ours. And worse,

in the long wakeful hours of darkness
memories cascade into consciousness,
pile up in logjams choking off sleep,
and leave me working my way
through the chaos of my mind,
dwelling on each memory for a time, then
casting it aside for another, rather like
you, browsing a bookshop's shelves,
looking for the perfect book.
Am I too, just looking
for the perfect memory?

Cat eating

I admire the cat for one thing.
She eats alone.
And just eats.
No need to catch the eye
of the diner opposite,
or make small talk,
or enjoy the presence of another.
She eats.

Without watching the television,
without reading a book or
that day's junk mail.
She just eats.
Then leaves.

But I can't leave.
I've been left.

Another poem about you

You always wanted me to write poems,
poems about you. (*'Yes!'*)
But you read the poems with some ambivalence:
you liked that I was focusing on you (*'Sort of...'*)
but you didn't like it that you were the focus of the poem,
since you wanted to see me published (*'Somebody has to!'*)
but not yourself revealed (*'No!'*).

Now that I am writing always,
and always about you (*'About fucking time!'*)
and more intimately than ever. (*'What? Can you elaborate – No, don't!'*)
It is somewhat unfortunate
that you're not here to keep an eye on me.
(*'You were just waiting for this moment, you bastard.'*)

Never fear, I have incorporated your perspective
in parenthetic remarks in this poem,
trust me. (*'Trust you? I'd as soon trust Donald Trump'*)
You always appear in a kindly light (*'Naturally'*),
I play the fool (*'That can't have been hard'*)
and, as always, I remain, yours faithfully. (*'You'd better!'*)

The presence of absence

The yellow sun finally slides
through the bedroom window
to fall first on the flat side of the bed
where you no longer sleep. As usual
I run my hand across the bedspread
to confirm this. No, you have gone.

The yellow sun looks weak. But
thirty-three is forecast. Even though
the equinox is expected next week. And
it is windy. A good day for washing.

I find no bras, knickers or T-shirts of a smaller size
in the wash. My clothes look lonely there. But
neither are the sweaty sheets that needed washing
every day or so. I never thought I'd miss those.

And in the lounge room there are no signs
of late night television watching. No two-thirds-empty glass,
perhaps a slightly crumbed plate, and a small blanket,
roughly cast aside. Nor are there the banked up half-filled
crosswords and sudoku, lifted from the past three days'
newspapers. Your absence is everywhere.

And yet the automatic part of my mind
refuses to see this – last night I still took
four pieces of cutlery from the drawer
when I only needed two. A slow learner?

Or does my unconscious recognise
your presence in all this absence?

Can we call this love?

glances that lock
and transmit secrets,
coded words and phrases
in public settings,
embraces, that last longer
than is socially appropriate,
kisses that shut out the world,
and other intimacies we allow
our bodies to engage in:
this we call love. But

moments of loneliness,
clouds of sadness,
passing showers of tears,
and emptiness, aching,
or the struggle
to put one foot in front of the other –
can we call this love?

I do.

My ex-wife

I know I should say my late wife – but
it wouldn't distinguish her from the living one.

She was always late –
in going out: 'You can't expect me to go out
without putting on lipstick or a bra or a more presentable top'
or at the front door,
'It's warmer or colder or wetter than I thought,
I'll have to go back and change
my slacks or jumper or coat or shoes.'

And coming in: 'I said to Caroline, Gaye or Jo,
"Goodness, is that the time?"' or
'Driving back from Northcote or Mooroolbark or Wollongong
took longer than I thought.'

Instead I say my ex-wife.
Who left me for another –
death made her an offer
she couldn't refuse.

And what could I say?

The woman who died

Susan Bell. I know that name.
I have it here, somewhere, on documents,
here: birth certificates; mother of a son in '72,
and mother of a daughter in '81 (she took her time),
a passport too, and credit cards. Her name fitted forms perfectly.

I accompanied her to consultations at Peter Mac
(someone had to know which way the trains ran
on the City Loop before and after one p.m.)
both in the pre-school atmosphere of the old
and the airline departure lounge of the new hospitals,
where a slightly unreal professor would emerge into
the glare of humanity and call 'Susan Bell? Susan Bell?'

I was married at the time,
to a lively woman named Sue Bell (no relation),
I haven't lost her, no, she's with me still,
a lovely woman who fills my dreams, both day and night
with past and imagined pleasures, and bears
no ill-will regarding my attentions to Susan Bell
who, unlike my Sue, really must be dead –

I have her death certificate.

You, the mother

The mother of our children.
is that how I best remember you?

There is some evidence –
the photos I have printed up tend to show
you with one child or the other.

Pressed in cross-examination I would plead
you were at your most beautiful then
– is that what I mean?

The children made you beautiful,
but we,
you and I,
made the children.

The colour of undying love

Yellow, bright yellow,
or sometimes a soft
and fading red.

It is nearing the end
of the second month of autumn
and the two forest pansy trees
in the side yard are losing leaves.

Large leaves, that float down
in the night, and at other times
when no one is looking.

You would pick them up
each year, slowly, carefully,
one at a time. Bending
from the hips, still
flexible, as they ever were.

We didn't know it then,
but yours was a dying love,
that paradoxically grew
stronger as death
neared. Now I am left
only with our undying love.

And these leaves, large
leaves, yellow, bright yellow,
and sometimes, a softly fading red.

The tears of autumn

Is autumn the best season?
It always seems so at the time.
Red spectrum colours come
and leaves go.

The sun is warm – not burning,
and an ageing body is grateful.
While the evenings are cool, the night is cold
which make sleeping a pleasure
rather than a hard-fought task.

Yet the season, for me, signifies loss.
I know yours was a summer death
but autumn always seems
the time for mourning, and the last flourish
of life before death,
made paradoxical by the promise
of the next generation, the apples,
the other autumn fruits, and the mushrooms,
pines and slippery jacks, relishing the cold
and the promise of rain. The tears of autumn.

Years ago, you and I,
in Rome on a September's night,
held close under an umbrella by the rain,
picking our way over the gleaming cobblestones
polished by the same rain, and thinking about dinner.
Not thinking about being
or not being.
Now I think about it all the time.

The invisible thread

When some read the poems
they said 'I never realised
you and Sue were that close'.
Neither did I.

I only see it now.
Our marriage was the invisible thread
that had strung together the fragments
of our life, like beads,
on the double helix of our love.

Now the thread is broken.
The fragments of our life
lie scattered across
the carpet of my memory.

I slowly bend to pick some up,
and carefully thread them
along the lines of a poem.
It takes time.

But I have plenty of that.

Is this day now just another day?

The sky is crowded with clouds in various shades of grey,
sun occasionally breaks through, but showers come and go
like tears. And the cold wind refuses to rip the last blossom
from trees. A picture of my mind in fact.

The wattle along the railway line has faded, fallen camellias
carpet the path in red and brown, and fresh green weeds grow
unchecked. My mind wants to wander through
memories of this day, your birthday.

But it can't. Has Death put a stop on memories of this day?
Perhaps not. In all our years there was only one poem
written on your birthday. And not a remarkable poem at that.
It could have been written any day. Perhaps this day
was always just another day. And any day
in our life together could have been remarkable.
Maybe I could celebrate the un-birthdays.
Or the half birthday. For you it falls on March the 15th.
The Ides of March, 'Beware the Ides of March'!

This is more like it. The ominous portent in your half birthday.
Me as Caesar, I see it now.
'Render unto Caesar the things that are Caesar's.'

I wish I'd thought of that and said it. You would have laughed
and said 'You need a shower. A cold shower.'

But if I had taken all the cold showers you suggested
I'd have died of pneumonia. Long before you.

And who would write birthday poems such as this now?

Bushfires

The Glenbrook fires have long gone.
They laid siege to our lives in sixty-eight
but were held – they retreated
leaving us an empty world –
and future memories.

Still warm grey ash underfoot
and black scars on my sleeves
where I brushed against a charred tree:
on this fire-emptied hillside,
no birds sing.

Your death was also such a fire
that swept through my mind so many years later.
Some fires cannot be extinguished.
This was one, I had to wait years
for the ashes of my anguish to cool,
and hope the phoenix of our life together
would rise again, in poems perhaps.

As then, slowly waddling across my path
in the post-fire devastation on that hillside,
a small and dusty, unthinking echidna
came from nowhere,
out of the cooling ashes.

The shock of love

A gift from nowhere
waiting for me on the table.
No birthday, nor Christmas nor Easter,
no, just a day, any day,
hastily wrapped
and you waiting.
Waiting to watch my reaction,
my initial shock – a present?
A present? For me? Why?
'I just felt like it,' you would say.
'Go on, open it.'

There would be a small crystal jug,
or a pair of liqueur glasses.
'I saw them in the op shop and thought of you.'
And all I could do was to kiss you.

Or some nights, you snuggled down into the bed,
watching me like a cat watches a wandering dove,
and as I'd pull back the bedclothes to get in,
I'd see you suddenly naked. You'd scream with laughter,
'You should see your face,' you'd say.
There was nothing for it but to turn out all the lights.

And in Rome in 1989, twenty years and two children
after our marriage. In the Hotel Regno on Via del Corso,
on our first day, grubby and sweaty from the flight.
I came into the room from second shower and
you were stretched out on the bed,
naked but for some minimalist lingerie bought in secret.
'You should see your face,' you laughed.
'It was worth every penny.'

It's your own fault

Some sunny Saturday mornings
we'd be lying peacefully in bed
until I'd say 'It looks as though
we'll be late for the farmers' market
this morning.'

And you would say 'It's all your fault.
If you hadn't attacked me…'
'Attacked you!' I would protest,
'I was sucked into the vortex of your
insatiable desire…' The argument
would continue until we both collapsed
laughing in an acceptance of joint culpability
for whatever had happened.

Then you'd say 'Well you'd better
have the first shower.
And make it quick.' And I'd complain
'But I had first shower yesterday,
It's your turn.' Then you would say
'It's your own fault. If you hadn't
attacked me… On second thoughts,
better make it a cold shower.'

Minutes later, clean and keen,
I'd leap back into bed to hear
'Ouch! Get away! You're freezing!'
And I'd say (trying not to laugh)
'But you did say a cold shower.
It's your own fault.'

If I were you

if I were you
and you were me,
we would be we,
not you and me.

Watching my granddaughter
at her final preschool music class
my eye is taken by two boys cheerfully
trying to strangle each other
with drumsticks. You would see it too.
'They're boys,' you would explain. Now
I must see it for myself. And wish
you were here. You would love it.

'I won't see my granddaughter grow up!'
Your first thought on the dreadful news.
And now you don't. Tears seem to be
my only solution.

On the road to nowhere

stumbling slowly
on the road to nowhere,
death is nowhere,
death is anywhere.

my body no longer moves
as I want it to, as it used to do,
with balance and purpose.
Now I am unsteady
my feet don't cope
with unevenness,
my ankles don't cope
with roll, and my knees
and hips don't cope with slope.

Purpose? There are
only immediate purposes,
a shopping list,
an appointment with coffee.

But not the drive towards
the unknown anywhere,
no, now there is
no drive, no unknown purpose
to push me forward
to the unknown anywhere.

Now there are only
the conscious drives, the known roads,
and the rest of my mind slowly
stumbles along on the road
to nowhere.

Anguish & despondency

When others gently inquire
if I've moved on,
I say cheerfully,
'Oh yes, I've moved on!'
(I used to be anguished,
now I'm despondent.)

When autumn turns to winter
and fallen fruit rot and turn to mush,
when crisp brown leaves become sodden
and collapse as dark sludge,
then the seasons match my mood,
and my world lies flat and empty.

When anguish burns itself out
and I am left with empty memories,
despondency rolls in like a fog,
blurring the shapes of things
that make up the landscape of my mind

until everything is nothing
and nothing everything.

Moving

In this house
you live still
I cannot see the space
but where you moved:
sliding into bed
rolling out of it (as late as possible)
and somewhere in between, stumbling
in the darkness
to the toilet.
Or in the morning
climbing awkwardly over
the bath's edge
to writhe in pleasure
under a hot shower.

And later, sitting still
with sudoku,
tea and toast,
movement because
there was none.

Then the 'housework':
moving smoothly
between vases, topping up water
and rearranging live blooms. Then
your finest movements:
adjusting your own appearance
in front of the mirror
before we could leave
the house for coffee.

You moved.
You move me.

Dreamcatcher

Some twenty years before your death
at a conference in Banff, Canada,
I bought you a souvenir dreamcatcher
at the native American store.

Maybe it worked –
but in your last years
it was a failure
for those night terror dreams.

Now I have need of a dreamcatcher
my dreams of the past,
the past with you,
are, yes, safely held

but the dreams of now,
the dreams of my future,
slip through
the spider webbing, and dissolve
in the darkness of the night.
I know not what
the future holds.

Busy being idle

'What are you doing
these days?' they ask.
'I'm busy,' I say,
'busy being idle.'

It's hard work being idle,
finding gaps in time
between the intruding tasks
of reality. Shopping is good,
carrying home the evening's alcohol
is so tiring I need a rest,
and a long, hard look at myself –
doing nothing.

For the rest, the household tasks
and the statistical analyses,
there is always the ten-minute break (every five minutes)
my personal union demands
and in which I can do absolutely
nothing. I love it.

And I'm good at it.
I've been practising
all my life.
My mother used to say
'Richard! Stop staring into space.'
My wife would more subtly say
'Earth to Richard. Earth to Richard.'

In theory I have less of it
these days. Sue, bless her heart,
had no time for idleness, which
left me to carry the load
for us both. Now I'm alone
it should be halved – but no,
there seems to be more
idleness than I can handle.

Now, I have to work nights as well,
coping with the backload,
lying awake in the dark hours
past midnight, a four-hour shift
doing nothing.
Insomnia? No, bliss.

Spring

The blue sky and warm sun
lift my spirits. In the side yard
the lilac points at the sky
with pale mauve fingers amidst
new flawless leaves,
and the adoring forest pansies
on either side slowly swap
tiny pink blossoms for
even smaller dark red leaves.

Life has come back.
For me too. My mind
has emerged from the Stygian gloom
of your death.
I feel like dancing.

Then my body chips in,
back, hips, knees, et cetera,
'Steady on old man –
and we mean old man,
we're no longer up for
living out your adolescent fantasies.
Besides, you don't dance.
Calm down for our sake.

If you must celebrate,
content yourself with
opening another bottle of prosecco.'

So I do.

The window seat

Whenever we took
the train, or come to think of it,
the plane, you commandeered
the window seat. Not that I minded.
On the plane I could stretch my legs more.
And on the train, well, I made those same trips
many times alone. I could be generous.

But now, you're no longer here
and I can take the window seat.
Though when I do on the train
and the carriage lurches,
I hit the window wall and my back
threatens yet another spasm.

I never realised
you only took that seat
to protect me.

And besides,
I could still sit alongside you,
feel the bone of your hip,
the warmth of your thigh,
and the soft bump of your shoulder,
as we rode the lurching train together.

Who needed a window seat?

Blood Moon, 5 a.m. 28 July 2018

This total eclipse of the moon,
starts on a clear early Melbourne morning,
slowly staining the bright white disc
with a red tinge like an old shiraz wine
spilt on a white damask tablecloth.
Or blood, dispersing in the waters of our life.

This cold night alone reminds me
of those times, when in love,
lust and blood tied us together
in such intimacy that is now
unbelievable, as when we succumbed
to one and coped with the other,

and I withdrew your bloody tampon,
replacing it with my cock,
that afterwards was equally stained
with that month's blood,
in our fairest exchange of fluids.

Oh love, never more
were we together
than in those moments.

Now, this bloody moon
stands alone with me
in such memories.

Gratitude

There was nothing
to look forward to,
so you looked back,
through your old diary,
letters and poems,
and took what pleasure
you could, in recollecting
our good times.

They were the best of times,
and if they were also the worst,
then the worst only made
the best better than the best.

When last you wrote to me,
on my birthday cards,
it was in gratitude
for those good times,

and now, I am writing,
I am always writing,
in similar gratefulness to you.

And not just for the good times.
The hard times, and the bad times
also made each of us, who we were
and who we are.

I am as much of you
as I am of me. Thanks,
R.

It is down to you – and my birthday

In the end the poems are down to you
– and my birthday.
If you hadn't had the PNET cancer you wouldn't
have been dying on my birthday in 2016.
If you hadn't been dying you wouldn't have
asked Alice to buy me a Readings book token
as your present. You'd have bought me a proper gift.

If you hadn't given me the book token with the weakest kiss,
I wouldn't have put it on the dresser
and forgotten about it. There were other things
to think about then. Like your suffering and death.

If I hadn't had a book token sitting on the dresser,
then, months later, I wouldn't have gone to Readings
to buy the forgettable book of supposedly imagist poetry
by that guy whose name I can't remember.
If I hadn't had to search for it on the poetry shelf,
I wouldn't have seen the book of excellent
funeral poems that I also bought
to exhaust the value of the book token.

If I hadn't thought that selection was excellent
then I wouldn't have gone out and bought some other
collections by the same editor. If I hadn't done that,
I wouldn't have seen a couple of poems by Sharon Olds.
And if I hadn't seen those, I wouldn't have bought some collections
of her verse just to see what her other poems looked like.

Then I wouldn't have owned her collection *Stag's Leap*.
If I hadn't read the poems there, I wouldn't have seen
the tone for my poems that I was looking for. And I would
not have written 'Such Sweet Sorrow' as I did.

So ultimately, yes,
it is down to my birthday – and you.

The last birthday cards

You played your last card
beautifully. The cover said
'Older, wiser & better than ever':
so you wrote 'And it's only been seventy-one years…
Still it's been worth the wait,
equally for me, with you.
Happy birthday Richard,
all my love, now & forever, Sue.
So much love & thanks
for all the years we've been together. Sue.'
It was the last time you wrote to me.

Was it better than the one you wrote in 2014,
just months after the diagnosis?
'My dearest Richard,
love is all you need.
And I have had forty-five years
of yours.
Thank you for those
and for the promise
of much more.
Love, Sue.'

Was it better? No, just harder
to read, harder in both senses of the word.
In 2014, your writing was still strong,
still the you we both knew. Two years later
you were far along the road to death,
your wrist was weak, and
the writing faint and feebly formed,

you were harder to read,
but it was still you.
I think I loved you more then.

And now, there's just me
and these two birthday cards.
It's not enough.

Lament

a world gone mad
a mind gone sad
what have things come to?

I wander through the garden
of my memories, pluck at a flower
here or there, or smell
the eucalyptus leaves, just
out of reach. It all comes back
to you. I've lost the sense
of touch that bridged the you
and the me, you are there,
somewhere, invisible,
beyond the sense of smell
and silent, not as the grave,
but as a love that does not need
to speak. I weep. We see not
shapes that once we saw instantly,
you, and me, now shadows both,
blurred and moving. You cry out
'But I won't see my granddaughter grow up!'
and I reach out, blindly,
for another memory, perhaps a dream,
anything to hold you here,
close in my mind, phantom in my arms,
together. Somehow.
Somewhere.
Sometime.

What works for you, works for me

I am so unformed
that any form of living
that works for you
will work for me.

You say you want freedom
and I say 'That's great. I love freedom.
What is it?'

You say you want to reach the stars,
to get away from this hard and struggling life.
Per ardua ad astra is my motto, I boast.

And then a rainbow makes your heart leap up –
'What a coincidence!' I cry.
'Me and Wordsworth went to school together.'

But next you say, 'I'm tired of me,
I want to be someone else,
someone strong and exciting,
with passion, love and caring.'

'You could be me,' I venture.
'Are you kidding?'
you reply.

In dreams

Dreams come like rain showers
sweeping across my mind
as they did across a sunlit Dartmoor,
going home from Exeter to South Zeal
forty years ago, home to you.

Now the dreams take me away,
away from you. My waking mind
can light upon your image, your words,
your smiles that also play upon my lips,
but the dreams, the dreams you feature in
(but never the one I'm waiting for),
take me away from the sunlit landscapes
of memories, drag me back to a wakefulness
that will be empty of you.

Then there's that last sleep –
perchance to dream? No,
the last sleep is the big sleep.
I don't need Marlowe to tell me
no dreams will thread their way
through that one.

The third autumn

Today was the first glimpse
of the coming winter.
Only the end of March,
barely a week since the equinox,
and yet today my hips ache.

This will be my third autumn
without you. Leaves are still green
and there's hardly any rain.
My tears have died now.

Yet there remains the loss.
An emptiness, now contained
in discrete private intervals,
can still command my mind.

I dither, pour myself another sangiovese,
and wonder, have I taken down
your photos, from the mantelpiece,
much too soon?

Emptiness is a winter feeling.
And winter is still two months away.

Where to now

Under a grey sky
and at the edge of the flat wet sand
the waves retreat. The tide goes out,
and with it, my dreams of today.
Night falls slowly. A white sea eagle
luminous in the fading light swoops
in long arcs and reminds me why
I am here, waiting for Godot's sister.

The night just rolls on.
Somewhere a dog is barking.
Not here, but there is always
a dog barking somewhere.
At something. Something that moves,
something that, perhaps,
is coming for me.
A rough beast –
or a smooth woman?
I cannot tell.

Or there is nothing –
the dog is making it up.

I sit on this bench of indecision.
To decide – or more likely,
not to decide. To remain
indecisive. To turn a somewhat
deaf ear to the plaintive cry
of the slow night train passing
through the half-lit city and across the river
into the land of lonely old men.
Instead I dream.

To wander through my mind

To wander through the empty streets
of my mind takes little effort.
Past empty shops of memories,
abandoned lots of cast aside ideas,
and darkened windows
of dreams that never were.

Houses, where once I lived, as a child,
adolescent or husband,
slip by without a wave, there
is no one home now. Knock-knock.
Who's there? No one. No one who?
No one who knows who you are.

The beaches we shared no longer
speak to me. Now I walk alone,
not 'together, but alone', just alone.
The endless shore and the waves
whisper to each other, as I trudge by,
moving slowly away from our past.

Grief is just another feeling

Grief is just another feeling
woven through fabric
of my life. As I run
the fabric through
my fingers of memory,
I feel the pain of losing you,
and the pleasure of holding you,
almost simultaneously.
Grief is both good and bad,
I would not have it otherwise.

Poems embroider themselves
upon this fabric.
Memories of what was,
or phantasies of what might have been.
They are no different.

I lived with you
and I live without you –
there is no difference.
There is a you and me
that goes beyond
what is. Or what
might have been.

Living and dying
are just vague descriptors
of our life together. And grief?
It's just another feeling.

The perfect metaphor for our love

at five thirty-four this morning,
lying there in the dark,
the perfect metaphor for our love
came suddenly to mind

we were two small araldite two-part glue
tubes, thick but runny emotions, useless alone
but stirred together –- a sudden strength.
I was the small red tube, you were the blue –
it matched your eyes.
But which was the adhesive,
which the hardener?
I still don't know –

but it held for forty-seven years.

It took death to pull us apart.

Tears and a yellow viyella dress

Cloudy, they say, a grey morning
followed by rain this afternoon.
I don't know I can wait that long –
tears threaten at breakfast.

Was it like this fifty years ago –
but that was in another country, and
besides, the wench is dead
no, I think not, though to be fair,
would I have known?
I was mesmerised by you
in your short yellow dress,
high hem and short sleeves –
the day must have been warm!

Though the material was viyella,
a wool-cotton blend that
is warmer than cotton,
maybe the day was cool – the dress was,
it looked grown-up and serious,
after all, you were
getting married. And so was I!

Now we are unmarried again. It's enough
to make a groaning man cry.
Start me up with tears
that now stain
an old yellow viyella dress.

1968

Watching the dusk from the Coogee cliffs
seeing it differently with someone else.

Sitting on the sharp white safety fence,
the setting sun blurred, lost its meaning:
yet I remember the white reflections
from across the bay, and the silver sea
pointed out to me.

The active joys replaced the passive –
sharply sang the walking along
the edge of wet sand around the curving bay,
and you, stopping to remove your sandals,
attractively awkward, ruining the soles of your stockings
while I collected dry sand in my shoes.

And at another time, we went to the gallery in Farmer's
where I had seen Blackman's Alice paintings alone and
was overcome – but beside you the Alice pictures paled.
I watched you wander down the gallery
and suddenly thought 'She is beautiful', scaring
myself. How much could Alice mean after that?

So we had to go back down to Pitt Street, I smiling,
as you held the hem of your short dress down
against the wind blowing up from the Quay.

The wilderness of love

found poem in Sue Green's prose journal

Tuesday 10 June 1969

Showed Julian's poetry to Richard.
Wonder why?
Richard, too, should try to publish his –
must start nagging him again,
he needs more confidence
but will encourage from afar I think
– it's much easier to have him now
as a friend, to want to change this

Must remember to stay clear of poets in future –
though, paradoxically
they're the sort of people I really click with.

Thursday 12 June 1969

Richard gave me his book of poetry to read yesterday –
just casually, out of the blue & so terribly naturally,
it was incredible.

After I'd wanted to read them for so long,
& then had really given up hope of ever doing so,
he just hands them over.
Was so astonished I didn't quite know what to feel
– so didn't think about it.

I must stop feeling or thinking about Richard.
if I do say something, I feel we must
step right through the barrier,
over the dividing line, into the wilderness of love.

The beginning

20 August (1969) Feeling vaguely drifting of late – as if something is about to happen & I don't know quite what. Impatient to find out and stabilise again. Sent out twenty-first invitations (kids variety) Except somehow it became a big thing in my mind as to sending Richard his invitation – really worried about what he'd think, whether he'd come, et cetera. And if he came, I'd be conscious all night of his being there & his watching me – for he would. Otherwise I'd be relaxed – so perhaps it's best if he does not arrive. I must wait and see.

Your party –- I remember agonising
over whether to come or not –
The last train home from Central left at ten,
so I would have to leave the party at nine-fifteen
or thereabouts. What time did twenty-firsts end?
I suspected nine-fifteen might have been a trifle early.

You said your family would put me up
but I'd never been to a twenty-first before –
or any party since I was ten. It would be strange
– but it seemed, however vaguely,
that you wanted me there.
Did I? There was something,
something I could sense but didn't know,
that drew me to say – eventually
Yes, I'll come – and stay the night – if that's OK.'

Friday 29 August Magnificent summer's day. Too beautiful to be perplexed by Richard. Saw him at U. yesterday & didn't know what to say to him – became terribly nervous & we said much more in eyes than words. When I first got his letter, went to jelly, wouldn't open it, couldn't, because I was so scared he wouldn't come. But Jen made me open it & he said he was coming & I was dazed, incredulous. Then followed a few days of whether he'd come & what he'd do, how he'd react. Knew I'd feel terribly conscious of myself, if he were there.

Then anxiety took over from indecision,
what if the book I'd bought
was also given by others? *The Beastly Beatitudes
of Balthazar B.* It would be so embarrassing
to see more of that stark white-lettered black book jacket.
And mine could not be returned, for I had written
a Walt Whitman poem in it.

A party outfit? I didn't have party clothes.
The thought of buying some never occurred to me.
It still doesn't. I wore an old brown nylon shirt,
the sort that showed sparks in the dark
and promoted perspiration, under a white sports coat
bought in a moment of madness five years earlier.
My pants were brown, a different brown,
I wore them to uni most days – they didn't show the dirt,
and my shoes – well, I only had one pair –
Hush Puppies (also brown).

I recall your outfit perfectly. Black short full skirted dress
(they all were short – I always appreciated that),
wide white modestly plunging V collar, white
cuffs and gold trim. I can see it now. It's easy,
I just go to the dressing room where it still hangs,
next to my unironed shirts.

Your hair; at the time you were growing your hair long
and it was at that halfway stage, wiry and unkempt –
but not that night, you had swept it up
with little ringlets dangling before your ears,
while you wore make-up – I'd never seen that before,
that perfectly took your face from beauty
to glamour for the night.
Stockings? – Oh no, I don't remember the stockings!
Maybe white. I was too scared to look at your legs.
And shoes, I don't remember them either,
but I do recall you changed them
when we went walking.

And earlier, anxiously walking
from Chatswood station to your home,
I had memorised the route –
but what if I forgot some part? It was dark
and there was no one to ask.

Light and noise flooded the front lawn,
the screen door was closed, I pressed
the doorbell. No one came. I was too scared to check
if it was locked. It wasn't. Eventually
a stranger came to the door and let me in.
Then I saw you, and that was it:
the beginning had begun.

The first of forty-eight

Every birthday was magical.
You wore celebrations so easily, both
the intimate and the public ones,
like the queen wears pearls. You loved parties.

But none were like the first, that twenty-first.
You went missing for hours. So did I.
There were more important things than parties.
We walked and talked and froze. It was bitterly cold.

We had been walking and talking for more than a year
but that night was different.
I took your hand at one point
to guide you past a puddle.
I'd never touched you before. I forgot to let it go.
The darkness seemed to hold us together.

We didn't notice at the time
 but that night we reshaped our lives
from thinking of ourselves as separate good friends
to thinking of ourselves as a couple,
not admitting it to others, or each other,
or even ourselves, but we were.

Monday 15 September Richard was a new person that night – forgetting himself as much as possible, leaving family amazed that they could talk to him so easily – I think I conveyed a wrong impression of him. But then the difficulty only arises in talking with him. But it wasn't difficult on Saturday night. He said I would be reprimanded for disappearing but I wasn't. Was missed, but people thought they understood. They didn't, but it doesn't matter. I don't really want them to. Though perhaps I would like to myself.

After the party: the thank-you notes

I was first cab off the rank,
firing in a thank-you note four days later
(anonymously of course)
Miss Green I have something
to tell you. It's brief.
Just to say
(new page)
Thank you.

To which you, I suspect laughing
as you saw through my anonymity,
responded
Mr Bell I have something
to add
You're welcome
p.s. thank you

But then you took the initiative:
Dear Richard,
Thank you for Saturday night
and Sunday morning.
For making my birthday perfect.
Love Sue.

Love? Love! It was the first time
that word had passed between us.
But two could play at that game – I replied,
Dear Sue
If I have helped make one day perfect for you,
it is because I enjoyed it.
But one day is not enough,
I would like to make them all perfect
for you.
Love
Richard
Take that!

And you did.

Tuesday 23 September and i think i am falling in love. Oh Richard,
all at once. And I am inundated & incredibly marvellously happy.
If a little frightened.

Blow Up

awoken it seems
by the loud rustling of those trees
before the wind

a sound
blown up to proportions
of sudden memories

of shortfalls in confidence
as stumbled words
rolled your body under bushes
and away again
faintly blue
in the clouded moonlight
and your nipples
dark as strawberries

hardly more than phantasy now

in this predawn light
green looks
float reproachfully
from the trees

I can almost believe
I dreamed it

I wish I had a camera

Quarrel

I hear the faint bells calling
as I go to the line and take down your warm towel:
even this bare concreted yard
is full of sun today.

Inside, your showering reflection twists and turns
under the steaming spray – you do not speak
and swing away.
I am left pink buttocks to contemplate,
and a curving back that slips and slims
to a narrow waist once clasped that
freely flared to hips I knew –
I turn away.

The rose that tore at my flesh in stealing drops petals –
turning back I see you bend for the soap
and your soft breasts swing in sorrow,
then straighten – to taste the bitter tears
of the fight that will last for days.

Now we are each alone.
You have barefooted gone
and I iron my shirts.

I'm driving, she said

we had
been drinking I think it was
champagne
and the unfamiliar roads
unfolded past the car
as I turned the pages
of the street directory

it was falling apart
we too felt that way
Sue I said let's stop
find out where we are
and where we're going
or

go home to bed
I added hopefully

but you changed up
from second
to third
grimly

and my hand
slid off your thigh

I remember

I remember the first time I saw you.
I don't remember the first time we spoke.
I remember you stamping your foot when vexed with me.
I don't remember when we exchanged poems.
I remember coming to your twenty-first birthday party.
I remember how beautiful you looked.
I don't remember the party at all.
I remember the first time we kissed.
It was a daring touch of lips in the hallway.
I remember we kissed until five a.m. next night.
I don't remember why we stopped.
I remember Centennial Park where we decided to marry.
My diary says it was three days after that first kiss.
I don't remember asking you to marry me next day.
Your diary said I did so it must be true.
I don't remember where I kept your great-grandmother's ring
while waiting the thirteen days to the marriage.
I remember seeing you in that yellow viyella dress
walking towards me, outside the registry office.
I don't remember anything of going to uni afterwards.
I remember your parents' shock when you burst in the back door,
a marriage certificate in one hand, a husband in the other.
I don't remember what your mother made for dessert that night.
I remember the fights we had.
I don't remember what they were about.
I remember when you told me you were pregnant.
I don't remember when you became pregnant.
People said it was when we were on a late summer holiday in Robe.
I remember we had to buy this house the moment you saw the marble fireplace.
I don't remember how I got you to agree to move to Perth soon after.

I remember the Crawley pier on hot nights, drinking cheap sparkling wine.
I don't remember what we did with our son.
I remember our wonderment on QF7 bound for London via Bombay.
Economy then was like Business class now.
I don't remember the interminable length of the journey.
I remember you buying that duffle coat on Tottenham Court Road.
Because of the cold – it was snowing.
I don't remember your second pregnancy.
But I have the photos. You glowed.

Aubade

We would lie close but not touching, held together
by the darkness, wishing night would never end –
it always did. The lights of the first morning train
would flicker across the far bedroom wall, as too slowly
autumn's night encroached on summer's dawn
and the seasons moved imperceptibly, as they always did,
towards the longer winter nights that I now long for.
I want darkness, that darkness which would then,
and will now, hold us together, close but not touching.

The predawn light slowly dissolves this black night,
the room turns to grey. Objects now loom
through the fog of fading darkness. The dresser
at the foot of the bed, our first piece of furniture,
the one to which I was going to affix
new handles to the drawers – I never did
and won't bother now, slowly sharpens its image.
An ugly shape that foretells of the night's ending,
knocked aside, trampled underfoot by an unruly sun.

Now we no longer lie together – you have gone.
Leaving me with just these memories
of you beside me – close, but not touching.
They will slowly shrink as time goes by –
but for now, like the scurrying of the last possum
along the back fence, and the frogmouth's freezing
into its daylight pose, they will disappear
behind the reality of the day's light, and alone
I will lie here in this growing light,
as you did in those last days, waiting,
as I sometimes wait now, for that last dawn,
the dawn that closes upon us all, day by day.

Flying to Istanbul

There is no comfort for an old man –
life and laughter, the marks of the young,
are now but seen in misted screen memories
that no longer refresh.

Perhaps I should take a plane
for noble Istanbul, there to find
meaning in an old beaten brass bowl,
sold to me oh so reluctantly
by an equally old woman while
her avaricious daughter clamours
for a better deal.

Or should I turn my mind
to fashioning phantasies of a newer life –
these old clothes then, they must go,
out with the old, in with the – the what?
What is new does not last,
the new is soon old – and was I ever that?

Flicking through images
of the past leaves me no choice:
the younger me was another man,
Love and laughter lived a different life then.
Such memories afford no relief –
I am trapped in a country of all old men.

And now the pestilence comes for me.
I hide behind this mask, lock down
my life, zoom into joyless contact
and wait. Time both slows and flies.
My clock is running down
and my time is running out.

While the old woman wraps
my brass bowl in old newspaper,
I look up at a blue-domed ceiling.
She is dreaming of eternity
in an enamelled heaven, and I –
I see my ending, coming to pass
as nothing more, nor nothing less,
than an old bowl of beaten brass.

Janus

Standing in the doorway
of love,
looking out and
looking in, seeing everyone
and seeing no one.

Looking back
there's much to see:
smiles and laughter
and rooms lit up
by your entrance.

Looking forward –
gloom dissolves
into distant darkness
concealing a future
of emptiness, sadness –
or even, another love?

Illusions

On an autumn evening when
dusk dissolves the blurred pink
the last of the sun's light in the pale
mauve of approaching night,
and the moon is full and rising
hugely behind the Dandenongs.
Suddenly it jumps into an empty sky.
There it shrinks, as does my interest.

I long for that immediate past where
my mind was full of that huge moon.
Just as when some special person
(yes, it was you)
came into a room and likewise
filled my thoughts and dreams
by being there, being seen, being.

Alas, the moon was not
as it had seemed to be. No,
there was no larger moon,
it was only as wide
as later at the zenith.
My eyes did not deceive me,
it was my mind.
The moon illusion they call it.

And perhaps those thoughts
of you were also just an illusion.
Were you then, and
are you now, just another person?

Fragment

It will be spring on arrival. In the park
bright new leaves of elm and oak
in adolescent green will match your eyes
for liveliness and life, and my words
will fall far short of the way
your pale hair moves
with the wind. You will smile,
lighting up my day – as the sun
breeds laughter on the grass.

I will push cheeky words
towards your careful smiles,
and tearful clouds will make their way
out of your life and mine, as we,
separately or together,
choose where our summer lies.

And at night, the still cold darkness
will push us each back into dreams
of this and other unknown regions.

Looming

A term from the psychology of perception, denoting an enlarging
image on the retina that the brain interprets as an approaching object.

Tunnel Mountain looms in my mind
as it once loomed in the dark pre-dawn
through my bedroom window
at that lonely conference. Slowly
taking shape in the growing light,
that memory, the absent you, then and now,
my present loneliness, all loom now large
and larger.

Back then there was answer: a walk
up the zigzag path on the side of the mountain,
that even then, twenty-four years younger, and fitter,
almost heart stopping and leaving me breathless,
as does this present moment without the physical effort,
or the view. I could see clearly then, across the Bow
River of no return, up the still snow-topped
Sulphur Mountain, and a path to the left,
perhaps a way out of the dilemma in my mind.
Sadly, I no longer have those resources,
I do not see clearly now.

That path, alone – I think I had the mountain to myself
that morning, skirting cliff edges, no safety fences there,
I found I had a head for heights, but no umbrella –
the rain came. Yet, on the right,
through the rain, the Hoodoos loomed.

Those ghostly white pseudo statues, carved
by the wind and tears of rain, from limestone,
moved as much as we did in difficult days, and now
it is the same, you no longer move, and I,
I find it almost impossible to move.

The only thing that moves now,
that looms, large and larger,
is loss and love,
looming as one.

As the rain falls

As the rain falls
I turn away from this
room full of memories
and focus on the simplicity
of this falling rain.

There is no purpose in it
the rain simply falls.
While I plot and plan and wonder
what my life will be,
the rain just falls.
Not often, this is Melbourne.
But sometimes.

And when it does
I put my thinking on hold
and just let my mind dissolve
in this falling rain.

9 781761 094125